WELCOME!

Welcome to the East Anglian Railway Museum. We give you an introduction to railway history in genera in particular. If you have any questions, please ask Visitor Reception.

EARLY RAILWAYS

The first railways started with horse drawn wagons, solely for freight: it was in 1801 that Richard Trevithick built his first locomotive in Cornwall. It was actually designed for travelling on road rather than rail, but it suffered an ignominious fate when it caught fire whilst he was in the pub! As early as 1802 the plan for East Anglia's first railway was put forward to run from Bury St Edmunds to Stowmarket, from where goods would be transhipped to barges that could then access the coast. In 1804 Trevithick's locomotive pulled a train of iron along a railroad in South Wales, although the cast iron track shattered under the locomotive's weight. It is, however, accepted that this was the first real railway locomotive, with 2004 seeing the bicentenary of the event and a number of special events being held across Britain.

East Anglia continued to see further plans put forward for railways, with the Norfolk & Suffolk Rail-Road proposed in 1824, planned to run from London to Norwich via Ipswich and Colchester with branches to Harwich, Bury St Edmunds, Great Yarmouth and Kings Lynn. In 1825 the Stockton & Darlington Railway was to open as the first public railway to use locomotives, which it was thought might be a spur to railway plans in East Anglia: on the contrary, in 1826 the planned Norfolk & Suffolk Rail-Road collapsed.

1830 saw the first public regular passenger service in the country, operating between Canterbury & Whitstable in Kent. In 1833 plans were announced for a railway between Ipswich and Bury St Edmunds (with branches to Lavenham and Hadleigh), but again this came to nothing. East Anglia's first railway was the Eastern Counties Railway, which was authorised in 1836 to build a line from London to Yarmouth via Ipswich, Colchester and Norwich: this was eventually opened as far as Colchester in 1843, before the money ran out.

RAILWAYS IN ESSEX: A BRIEF CHRONOLGY

1839	The first railway opened, between Mile End and Romford
1840	The line was extended at both ends, and now ran from Shoreditch to Brentwood
1843	The line was extended from Brentwood to Colchester
1846	Colchester, Stour Valley, Sudbury & Halstead Railway incorporated
1849	The line from Marks Tey to Chappel and Sudbury was opened

1860	16 April: Colne Valley Railway opened from Chappel to Halstead, and extended in stages to Haverhill, reached on 10 May 1863
1862	The Great Eastern Railway was formed, and took over the running of the majority of East Anglia's railways
1865	9 August: Sudbury – Long Melford – Haverhill opened, as did Long Melford to Bury St Edmunds
1865	(Cambridge) – Shelford – Haverhill opened
1894	Liverpool Street Station suburban platforms opened
1895	Liverpool Street station main line platforms opened
1923	The Great Eastern Railway was absorbed into the London & North Eastern Railway (LNER), as was the Colne Valley & Halstead Railway
1948	Britain's railways were nationalised: East Anglia's services came under the Eastern Region
1959	Diesel multiple units replaced steam on many of East Anglia's lines
1961	10 April: Long Melford to Bury St Edmunds closed to passengers
1962	1 January: Colne Valley railway (Chappel – Halstead – Haverhill) closed to passengers
1963	Dr. Beeching's Reshaping Plan was published, which spelt the end for many branch lines
1963	28 January: most intermediate stations between Marks Tey and Cambridge had staff withdrawn, including Chappel
1964	2 November: Freight facilities at Chappel withdrawn
1965	19 April: last freight train (Colchester) – Chappel – Halstead
1965	Closure notice posted for Marks Tey to Sudbury line
1967	6 March: the line from Sudbury to Haverhill and Cambridge was closed
1986	Network SouthEast was set up, with many lines in Essex coming under Great Eastern brand name
1991	Great Eastern became a division of Network SouthEast
1997	Under the privatisation process, the Great Eastern franchise was awarded to FirstBus
1998	FirstBus change their name to FirstGroup and, with it, Great Eastern becomes First Great Eastern
2004	The franchise changes hands, with Great Eastern becoming operated by National Express

WHY CHAPPEL IS HERE

When the line from Marks Tey to Sudbury was built between 1846 and 1849, it was designed to link Sudbury with the main line to London and Colchester at Marks Tey, and to continue on from Colchester to the Hythe.

This would give access to the port of Colchester – which was then a much busier place than it is today.

Chappel and Wakes Colne were adjacent to the line, hence the provision of a station here. With roads at that time very poor, the coming of the railway opened up whole new markets to local farmers: hence the provision of goods yards at virtually every station. The Goods Shed at Chappel is an excellent example of how goods arrived and were loaded: carts were backed up to the big doors on the east side of the shed, and their contents were off-loaded and into the waiting wagons.

With the opening of the Colne Valley & Halstead Railway in 1865, Chappel became a junction station, and assumed greater importance. Whilst some trains from the new line ran through to Marks Tey and Colchester, others terminated at Chappel which therefore saw passengers changing trains. Freight traffic too was increased, which meant more shunting and more sidings were created.

During the Second World War an oil depot was established at the station, on land which is now occupied by new housing adjacent to the Museum's main entrance drive. Aviation fuel was then distributed from here to the many local airfields, including those at Wormingford and Earls Colne. In the first six months of 1944 no less than 103 special trains of petrol were received at Chappel.

After the war, road transport played an increasingly bigger part in the movement of both freight and passengers, and some of the facilities at Chappel gradually became disused. The publication of the infamous Beeching Report in 1963 recommended that both the lines that served Chappel should close: in the event, the line to Halstead and Haverhill closed in 1962, and the line from Sudbury to Cambridge closed in 1967. Despite the strenuous fight to retain the Marks Tey to Sudbury section it was anticipated that this too would close: hence when the lease of the station site became available the then Stour Valley Railway Preservation Society moved into the site in 1968.

The station buildings from the station approach, pictured in May 2004

A TOUR AROUND THE MUSEUM

Welcome to the East Anglian Railway Museum, officially opened in its present form on 19th August 1986 by Dr. John Coiley, then Keeper of the National Railway Museum, York. Here, at the original Victorian country junction station of Chappel & Wakes Colne, the past is being kept alive with the most comprehensive collection of nineteenth and twentieth century railway architecture and engineering in the region. This is a 'working' museum allowing visitors to see the actual restoration work in progress, from re-upholstering seats and wooden coach building to heavy engineering overhauls on steam locomotives. It is open every day (except Christmas Day) with all the locomotives, rolling stock and buildings available for inspection, whether restored, undergoing renovation or awaiting attention. If you are here on an Operating Day you will also have the opportunity to see some of the vehicles in action and to enjoy unlimited rides behind one of our steam or diesel locomotives.

The East Anglian Railway Museum is an entirely independent charitable organisation devoted to preserving our regional railway heritage. The Museum effectively started in 1968 when a small band of railway enthusiasts formed the Stour Valley Railway Preservation Society with the object of saving part of the former cross-country rail link from Colchester to Cambridge, which had already been cut back to Sudbury. With this remaining service also due for withdrawal, the

The station buildings in 1974, before the Museum erected the footbridge and relaid the track in Platform 2

Society set up headquarters at Chappel & Wakes Colne Station, then used by British Railways as an unstaffed halt only. A lease was obtained on the unused buildings and goods yard which would become the operating and maintenance depot if the Society was successful in acquiring the line after closure. In anticipation of this event a collection of locomotives and rolling stock were gathered at the site along with signalling equipment, extra track and all the other items necessary for running a railway. To draw attention to the project and help pay the running costs of the depot, Steam Open Days were held at regular intervals for the public to explore the site and ride behind steam locomotives.

Over the years, however, the threat of closure receded, so efforts were concentrated on developing the site into a working museum. With the help of the Manpower Services Commission major works have been carried out with this object in view, including the erection of a large restoration and display shed. The site which had variously been known as Chappel Steam Centre and the Stour Valley Railway Centre was re-launched as the East Anglian Railway Museum after completion of this building. In 1989 the basement area beneath the station was cleared and converted into a Visitor Reception area.

In 1991, the Museum was able to complete the purchase of the site from British Rail after an appeal was successful in raising the necessary funds, thus assuring a secure future at Chappel. This was followed in the same year by the Museum becoming a registered educational charity with the aim of educating all, not just the young. The Museum continues to receive no funding from any central organisation, relying in the main on income from visitors to the Museum and from members' subscriptions.

Great Eastern still operates a regular service between Sudbury and Marks Tey (connecting there for stations to Colchester, Clacton, Ipswich, Chelmsford and London), which calls at Chappel & Wakes Colne. It was announced in Autumn 1994 that as part of an economy drive the Summer-only Sunday service that had previously operated from May to September each year would not operate in 1995; urgent discussions and a substantial underwriting commitment by the local Councils saved the Sunday service for 1995 but the threat to the service in future years still persists. At present the service operates seven days a week all year round. Regardless of the outcome, the East Anglian Railway Museum site at Chappel will continue to be developed and improved for the benefit of public and members alike.

THE VISITOR RECEPTION

Following the relaunch of the Museum in 1986, efforts have focused on the restoration of the unique collection of locomotives, coaches, and wagons dating from the 1870s onwards. It was soon realised that, in order for the visitor to appreciate both the work of the Museum and, more importantly, the history of the railways of the Eastern Counties, an introduction to the site and collection was needed. The Visitor Reception area was planned using the space under the station buildings. With the demise of the Manpower Services Commission and their Community Programme

The Visitor Reception has a wide range of books, gifts and souvenirs available

schemes, the Museum set itself up as an Employment Training provider, a result of which was all the necessary building and joinery work was carried out by trainees under the supervision of two supervisors employed by the Museum. Funding for such a major project was a prime consideration, but fortunately the East Anglia Tourist Board provided a 20% grant towards the cost and a small grant was made by Eastern Electricity. The Centre itself was opened on 16th August 1989, almost three years after the Museum itself, by Rob Shorland-Ball, Deputy Keeper of the National Railway Museum at York. With its audio-visual facilities, complete disabled access, and all year-round comfort, the Heritage Centre became a major feature of the Museum. The displays were centred on the twin stories of the Museum and the passenger and freight traffic on the country railways of East Anglia during the one hundred years ending with the Beeching cuts of the 1960s. These, in turn, prompted the formation of the voluntary organisation that now runs the Museum.

THE STATION BUILDINGS

The station buildings are a splendid example of Victorian architecture with an unusual exterior double staircase leading to the Booking Hall. In the former Booking Office you can take a look at the Great Eastern Railway crest cast into the fireplace. To the other side of the booking hall is the former general waiting room, which is now a meeting room with some exhibits: adjacent to this is the former Ladies waiting room and toilets: this room is now used as the Museum Curator's office. Turning left onto the adjacent Platform 1 (which is used by Great Eastern's Marks Tey to Sudbury train service), you will pass the Station Master's Office, which is nowadays used for administration of the Museum. Next to this are the Gents and Ladies toilets with a storage room in between the two. This storage room was originally used for the storage of lamps and lamp oil -every signal would have had an oil lamp for illumination at night, a practice that still continues on some rural lines today. The Station Master's house which was the original Station is the last building alongside the platform and is now privately owned. Finally, just beyond the platform outside the station is the Old Railway Tavern which is now the home of a member. Of interest is the original engraved glass in the door nearest to the platform.

THE ORIGINAL (MAIN) SIGNAL BOX

A short distance from the end of Platform 1 is the original signal box dating from around 1890. This controlled the operation of the station and yard before the Sudbury line was reduced to a long siding in 1967, when all passing places and local sidings were removed. Chappel had two operational platforms, and trains passed here and connected with the Colne Valley line to Halstead and Haverhill. This box is owned by the Museum but cannot be utilised because it would require rodding and wires to pass beneath the Network Rail track. Instead, it has been renovated and equipped as a signal museum, allowing visitors to pull the levers, examine various telegraph instruments, and learn something of the operational procedures when Chappel was a busy junction. It is also possible to obtain a signalman's eye view of the Great Eastern trains that still serve the station, linking the Museum to the railway of today.

PLATFORM 2 AND SIDINGS BUFFET

Return along Platform 1 and cross the footbridge. This footbridge was originally at Sudbury Station and was dismantled and re-erected in its present position by volunteer members. The track in Platform 2 was also re-laid by the Museum. This is where the Buffet is located and from which light meals, snacks and refreshments are available on event days throughout the year (on non-event days, drinks and confectionery are available in the Visitor Reception). The coach body on the platform is at present used for the sale of second hand books and magazines, but there are long term plans for it to be restored and united with a set of wheels. The buildings that were formerly on Platform 2 were razed to the ground in the nineteen sixties, prior to our occupation of the site. Continue along Platform 2 towards the level crossing, past the station gardens that were a feature at all country stations. From the level crossing, you will see the

GOODS SHED

Restored to its 1891 condition, this historic building demonstrates the reason for the early railways, the handling of freight and trans-shipment of goods. Now it is used for a wide range of special events, displays (including a fine selection of railway signs) and exhibitions, with the former clerk's office housing the Small Exhibits Museum. The wooden crane inside, which came from Saffron Walden Goods Shed, was rebuilt by a Museum member, and completed in 1992. The Goods Shed was used to store items before being unloaded from road vehicles and reloaded by hand or using the crane in the shed. A daily freight train – sometimes more than one ran – would arrive at Chappel, and various wagons would be attached and detached. This was known as the 'pick-up freight'. Loaded trains ran between the main marshalling yards – where the wagons were sorted according to their final destination before going forward on other trains. The two best known ones in East Anglia were at Temple Mills (near Stratford in East London) and at Whitemoor (at

The Goods Shed, pictured in May 2004

March in Cambridgeshire). The Goods Shed is available for hire for functions: please ask at the Visitor Reception for further details. Leaving the Goods Shed, you will see

PLATFORM 3 (CHAPPEL HALT)

This is a re-creation of the typical East Anglian country halt, once so much part of the railway scene. It has been built using materials from many closed stations, including a cast iron Gents toilet from Cockfield on the former Long Melford to Bury St. Edmunds line. Passenger trains usually depart from this platform on Operating Days, giving a nostalgic reminder of days long past.

Platform 3 during a quieter moment during one of the Museum's regular 'Day out with Thomas' events

RESTORATION SHED AND WORKSHOP

Adjacent to Platform 3, this was built with the help of the Manpower Services Commission in 1983-5 to provide facilities vital for the restoration and maintenance of locomotives, rolling stock and equipment. Toilets have also been included in this building. Most of the materials and components for the structure came from the sheds erected to house air compressors during the construction of the second Dartford Tunnel, with the brick facings coming from the former Goods Shed at Witham. A steady programme of upgrading has continued; much of the floor of the restoration shed was concreted in 1993 (formerly it was an earth floor) and new improved lighting was installed in 1994. The preservation teams can normally be seen at work and are only too willing to answer questions about their various tasks. We regret that access to the machine shops is not normally available due to safety requirements and would ask that you take care whilst walking around the restoration shed.

Chappel North Signal Box

CHAPPEL NORTH SIGNAL BOX

This signal box controls operations at the Museum and is situated at the end of Platform 3 and on operating days visitors have the rare opportunity of seeing a signalman at work. This building was formerly located at Mistley, on the Manningtree to Harwich line, and is believed to date from the 1880's. It was rendered surplus to British Rail's requirements when the Harwich branch was electrified but was saved from demolition by being brought to Chappel by the Museum in December 1985. It was renovated and re-erected on its present site and immediately brought into service. Due to natural decay, it was found necessary to replace the steps in late 1994. It is a Grade II listed structure.

MINIATURE RAILWAY

Walking from the Restoration Shed, alongside the orchard, you will see the Miniature Railway. This runs on most Operating Days, and offers passenger rides at a small supplementary charge. Work started on this in its present location in 1991, and it operates on two different gauges. It also has its own small ticket office and engine shed. A programme of extending the line towards the south of the Museum's site is at currently under way.

CHAPPEL SOUTH SIGNAL BOX

Carry on walking south past the end of the Miniature Railway, heading towards the viaduct, and another smaller signal box will be seen installed. This was from Fotherby Halt in Lincolnshire and is used for controlling access to the

A diesel loco operating on the miniature railway - steam locos also operate as well.

sidings during shunting. It was located at the north end of the Museum site for many years, and soon after being displaced by the signal box from Mistley it was taken to Windsor Safari Park where it featured in a drinks commercial. It is not normally used when trains are operating, but can be staffed to demonstrate the use of single line instruments and bell code communication between signal boxes.

THE SIDINGS

Returning from Chappel South Signal Box towards the Goods Shed, you will see the sidings. Visitors are encouraged to explore this area and inspect any vehicles or other equipment that may be of interest. In the past few years there has been some rationalization of the Museum's collection, in order to concentrate as far as possible on our aims of preserving East Anglia's railway heritage: some vehicles have been donated on to other museums. Most vehicles carry brief information on them, and full details can be found in the Museum's Stock Book, on sale in the Visitor Reception. Please remember that there will be dirt and grease about, so care should be exercised to avoid coming into contact with it and to watch out for any trip hazards. Also, you are respectfully requested to comply with any notices that may be displayed for safety reasons and are asked not to enter any fenced off areas, especially on Operating Days. Returning past the Goods Shed, cross the level crossing and continue along Platform 2. After visiting the Buffet, you can return via the footbridge to Platform 1 and the station buildings.

Don't forget to revisit the Visitor Reception before you leave, to browse through the wide range of railway books, information, toys, gifts and souvenirs to be found in there. If the book you want is not in stock, we will be happy to order it for you. An increasing amount of these items are also available for sale on line from our web site, http://www.earm.co.uk

CHAPPEL VIADUCT

Although outside the main area of the Museum, the viaduct over the River Colne is a feature of such magnitude that it never fails to impress. It is the largest viaduct in East Anglia, and was opened in 1849, after less than three years construction, despite containing seven million bricks. With thirty two arches and a total length of 1060 feet, it stands seventy feet above the valley it spans, with the Museum at the north end. If you have the time to spare, why not take a trip on a train to Marks Tey and back, crossing the viaduct? The round trip takes thirty minutes, and tickets should be purchased on board the train. For information on the train times, please ask at the Visitor Reception.

Chappel Viaduct seen from the Millenium Green

LOCOMOTIVES

Apart from individual numbers and classes, locomotives are further identified by the number of wheels. This system uses the Whyte notation, listing in sequence the number of small carrying wheels at the front, the number of driving wheels, and then the carrying wheels to the rear.

Steam Locomotives

All the steam locomotives at the Museum were used on industrial rail systems in quarries, foundries, paper mills or power stations. The steam locomotives are all of the Saddle Tank design in either 0-4-0 or 0-6-0 wheel arrangements. Of these 0-6-0 **'Pen Green' No.54** (Robert Stephenson & Hawthorn, works No.7031) and 0-4-0 **'Jubilee'** (Bagnall, works No.2542) have seen extensive service on Steam Days at the Museum in recent years, although both are at present out of service for overhaul. Other steam locomotives include 0-6-0 **'Belvoir'** (Andrew Barclay, works No. 2350), 0-4-0 **No.11** built in 1905, the oldest locomotive at the Museum (Andrew Barclay), 0-4-0 **'Birkenhead'** (built by Robert Stephenson and Hawthorn in 1948, works number 7386), 0-4-0 **'William Murdoch'** (built by Peckett in 1948) and 0-4-0 **No.2039** (Peckett). The last engine has been named **'Jeffrey'** and, with a face painted on the smokebox, proves very popular with children.

No.11 on the Museum's demonstration line in May 2004

Diesel Locomotives

Moving to the diesel locomotives, we start with 0-6-0 diesel shunter No.**D2279**, built by Drewry in 1959. One of British Railways Class 04, it was originally allocated to the Southern Region but was later transferred to the Eastern, ending its days under BR ownership at Colchester. After a period of use by the Central Electricity Generating Board, it was privately purchased and brought to Chappel in 1981.

In addition there are two further diesel shunters, 0-4-0 No. AMW144 (Andrew Barclay, works No. 333 and 0-4-0 **No.23** (Fowler) ex-Shell Haven refinery, the latter normally appearing as a licensed replica of 'Toby' from the 'Thomas the Tank Engine' © characters.

Class 04 diesel locomotive D2279 at rest outside the Restoration Shed in May 2004

Diesel Multiple Units

Diesel multiple units are also to be seen at the Museum, with two types of the British Railways 1950's Modernisation Plan First Generation DMUs on site. **E50599** is a **Class 108** Driving Motor Brake Second built by British Railways Derby workshops in 1958. It is an example of the final series of 'Derby Lightweight' DMUs and arrived at Chappel in July 1993. DMBS **E51213**, DMCL **E51505** and DTCL **M56358** are Class 101 DMUs built by Metropolitan Cammell, Birmingham in 1958 and 1959. The last examples of the class continued in passenger service until 24th December 2003. E51213 and M56358 were regularly used on the Sudbury branch between 1974 and 1994, before being transferred to Manchester; they were withdrawn from passenger service by June 2001. They were purchased in September 2003 and arrived at the Museum in October 2003. E51213 and M56358 re-entered passenger service at the Museum on 14th March 2004.

The introduction of DMUs proved to be the saviour for some branch lines as it enabled the withdrawal of station staff, with the guard collecting the fares on the train. These vehicles represent the types of DMU that were used on rural branch lines for over forty five years from the late 1950's onwards, including the Sudbury Branch.

Further details of all these items will be found in the Museum Stock Book, available from the Visitor Reception.

Class 101 No. 51213 pictured in Platform 2 at the Museum early in 2004

GOODS WAGONS

Nowadays, with the majority of rail freight being transported in containers on Freightliner trains, one is apt to forget the vast range of goods trucks of many shapes and sizes that plied our railway system only a few years ago. Of these some were fitted with automatic continuous brakes, but many were marshalled into loose coupled trains relying on a brake van at the end of the train to supplement the locomotive's stopping power. There are two brake vans at Chappel, No.**B951771** of British Railways standard design, and No.**17898** from the Great Western Railway, known by the code name 'Toad', the latter currently being overhauled. Both vehicles are regularly included in demonstration freight trains at the Museum with passengers permitted to ride in the 'Toad'.

The collection at Chappel includes three tank Wagons of which **No. 2** was built for the West Midlands Sugar Company in the mid-twenties to transport molasses. The remaining two, Nos.**5474** and **5478** were for carrying fuel oil and generously donated by BP, the former having already been fully restored. 5478 has been restored to the rare wartime POOL livery and is now located at the front of the station. Enclosed Vans are represented by No.**32518**, a Great Eastern 10 ton ventilated van; No.**E765W**, a BR Special Cattle Van; **No. 1152,** a Southern Railway Parcels/ Mail Van; No.**B760651**, a BR Box Van; and **No. 3,** a mobile workshop van for Pooley's who maintained weighbridges and other weighing apparatus on the Great Eastern Railway. This last vehicle, which became L.N.E.R No.**96710**, was used to give passenger rides at Chappel in the early days of the preservation era. In addition, 12 ton Cattle Truck No. **B892156** (one of only three remaining examples), which was built at Swindon in 1950, has been on loan from the

Special Cattle Van No. E765W

National Railway Museum for some years but early in 1995 it was decided that Chappel would become its permanent home and it was donated to the Museum. Apart from the above there are two bolster wagons, an LMS wooden 5-plank open wagon (No. **M405032**, which is fitted with seats), an LNER fish van (No. 159918), a 12 ton steel open wagon No. **B745522**, a van chassis, an LMS hopper wagon No. **691762**, a Covered Carriage Truck No. **S1439**, and two 16-ton mineral wagons, one of early vintage (No. **B68231** built in 1951) and one of the later designs (No. **DB437781** built in 1957). There is also a Tube wagon No. **B732205** which was built to carry steel: this is currently being overhauled and having seats fitted and will be used in our popular demonstration freight train when completed.

VINTAGE COACHES

One of the specialties of the East Anglian Railway Museum is a collection of (mainly Victorian) passenger coaches, most of which were of Great Eastern origin. When acquired, such vehicles had long since disappeared from active service and were usually found languishing in the guise of holiday homes, chicken sheds or put to other equally undignified uses. All are wooden bodied and many were without wheels or running gear when they originally arrived at Chappel: an example of this is ex-GER Third Class Brake built in 1873, No. **TB308**. It was withdrawn from service in 1902, and was used for many years as a chapel at Great Wenham (near Ipswich) before arriving at the Museum in 1988. This is now located north of Chappel North signal box and is at present used for a permanent way store.

G.E.R. **No. 19** is a 4-wheeled coach built in 1878. Wheels, springs, axle boxes and other essential components were accumulated from a variety of sources

No.19

to enable this one-time beach chalet from Felixstowe to be returned to its former glory as a fully restored railway vehicle for first class passengers.

Coach **No.704** (L.N.E.R. No. 60704) had six compartments for third class passengers and currently rests on Platform 2 where it functions as a shop selling second hand books, magazines, etc. This will be restored in due course.

No.553 is a six-wheeled G.E.R. passenger brake van dating from 1890 designed for main line use and withdrawn in 1934 as L.N.E.R. No. 63761. Its first appearance in restored condition was at the 150th anniversary celebrations for the opening of the Eastern Union Railway to Ipswich in 1996. Restoration of this vehicle is nearing completion and it will eventually form part of the Museum's vintage train. Another vintage vehicle is a late Great Eastern bogie coach

No.E61533E, dating from 1921. This had been in use as a Mess Room at Boston (Lincolnshire), and was acquired from British Rail in 1988. At present, restoration, which will be a major job, has yet to commence but it is hoped that work will begin soon. The original appearance of this vehicle is well preserved.

The most recent of the vintage fleet is ex LNER Open Third **No.13251**, built in 1936. Formerly at the National Railway Museum, this vehicle moved to Chappel in 1995 and has just started a period of lengthy restoration. It is anticipated that restoration of this coach will be completed in 2007: restoration of vintage coaches being a long and time-consuming process.

BRITISH RAILWAYS BUILT COACHING STOCK 1948 TO DATE

The Museum is host to several relatively modern steel-bodied passenger coaches built during the 1950's for British Railways, all of which are fitted with vacuum brakes, which have now been largely superseded by air operated systems on current Mk1 coaches. The earliest arrival at Chappel was the Suburban Brake

Mark 1 coaches numbers E24959 and M21027

No.E43157. This was a standard BR non-corridor design with six full-width compartments each seating twelve second-class passengers, plus a guard's compartment with luggage space. Throughout its life with British Railways it operated on services within the King's Cross suburban network. Full restoration of the bodywork and underframe was completed late in 1994, with interior restoration completed in spring 1995. Three British Railways Mark 1 main line coaches are included in the modern vehicle stock. **No.E24959** is a Corridor Second (SK) with eight compartments each seating six second class passengers, and a side corridor. **No. M21027** is a Corridor Brake Composite (BCK) seating twelve first class and eighteen second class passengers. This also has a side corridor and guard's compartment with luggage space. These two vehicles have been extensively used for Steam Day rides since 1985. The other Mark 1 coach is Tourist Second Open (TSO) **No. E3779** containing 64 seats (two a side with tables): this coach is normally in Platform 2 to provide seating for our catering unit.

CRANES

Cranes are essential for any form of heavy lifting and are well represented at the Museum. There is a rail-mounted steam-driven crane, donated by the Felixstowe Dock & Railway Company, built in 1914 by the Grafton Engineering Company of

The steam driven crane generously donated by the Felixstowe Dock & Railway Company

Bedford and capable of lifting 4 tons. This was often to be seen at work moving heavy materials in connection with the Museum's restoration programme, or giving demonstrations of freight handling but is undergoing major boiler work before returning to service. This is supplemented by a diesel-electric road crane, previously in British Railways ownership and typical of the type used in Goods Yards through-out the country: this is currently being overhauled. Close to the viaduct end of the Goods Shed a fixed hand-operated Yard Crane (Kirkstall Forge, Leeds 1865) has been installed. When this type is utilised, the wagons waiting to be loaded or unloaded are moved up to the crane in turn, where the cargo is transferred to or from a road vehicle. Wagons were originally shunted about the yard by horses, which were housed in a stable block located near the Goods Shed; this was demolished in the 1960's due to its dangerous condition. The last crane is wooden and performed a very similar function but was fixed to a wall inside the Goods Shed. This particular example is from Saffron Walden and also dates back to Victorian times, and has been fully restored.

ODDMENTS AND CURIOSITIES

Rather strange in appearance is a small rail-mounted petrol-driven car, designed to transport track maintenance gangs to the scene of operations. More conventional platelayer's transport is represented by petrol-driven **Wickham** trolleys. These are basically small flat trucks each with a roof and an engine. Trolleys are intended to be removed from the track when not in use so it might be difficult to find these vehicles on some occasions. A **pump trolley** is also to be found at the Museum. This hand operated 'machine' is powered by a minimum of two people pumping up and down on a central handle, and was used to transport permanent way staff to the scene of work - as well as being made famous in one of the St. Trinians' films! It is used for demonstration runs several times each year.

The Museum's pump trolley

The Museum is also host to one steam-driven road vehicle, Aveling & Porter 'D' class **steam roller No. 12462**. This was built in 1921 and worked for Essex County Council during the 1950s.

A WORD ABOUT THE TRACK

Usually overlooked or totally disregarded by visitors, track nevertheless forms the major part of any railway system. Most of the rails at Chappel had been lifted at the time the site was first occupied by the Stour Valley Railway Preservation Society so over the years track has been obtained from many sources including redundant factory sidings as well as surplus British Railways material. Consequently, a wide variety of rails and fittings can be seen at the Museum. The tracks used by passenger trains and most of the sidings are constructed from **bullhead rail** which is fitted in chairs with wedges or springs known as keys. In the Restoration Shed, however, the lines are laid in **flat bottomed track** which has a wide lower flange enabling the rails to be clamped straight down onto concrete sleepers. Some of the lines leading to this shed are also flat bottomed but are spiked down onto wooden sleepers. There is a display of permanent way items close to the level crossing.

FINISHING TOUCHES

The main object of the East Anglian Railway Museum is to recreate the atmosphere of the steam railway era, and to this end many details have been added to give an air of authenticity. Briefly, some of the more noteworthy items are:
- A collection of enamel advertising signs distributed around the site, but particularly on the railings behind Platform 2 and on the wall adjacent to Platform 3. Most of these are genuine original articles which have been carefully restored.

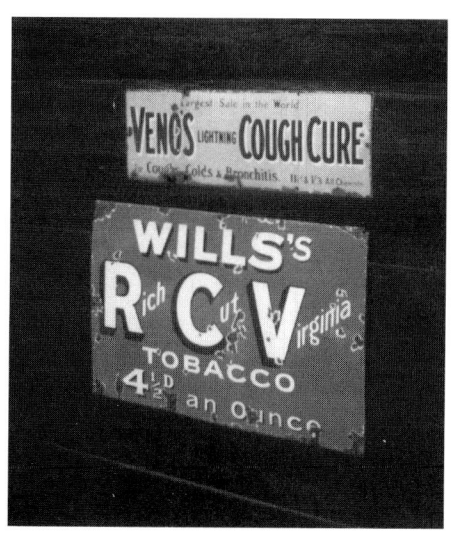

Just some of the enamel signs to be seen around the Museum. Most of these signs can be found on Platforms 2 and 3 and in the Goods Shed.

- A collection of luggage - suit cases and trunks - to recall the heyday of holidaying by train. These are located in the Booking Hall and in the Goods Shed.
- Platform trolleys and milk churns are usually to be seen in various locations.
- The water crane near the end of Platform 3 was originally installed at Great Dunmow station.
- The flower beds on Platform 2 were created to brighten up an otherwise rather austere part of the Museum site, and recall a typical feature of most country stations.
- The lamp standards on Platforms 2 and 3 are of a fairly typical design for stations blessed with electricity.

One of the Museum's platform lamps: these were once common place on many stations

We want all our visitors to enjoy their visit to the Museum; if you have any questions, please feel free to ask any of our working volunteers about any aspect of the Museum. If they don't know the answer, they normally know someone who does!

FACILITIES FOR DISABLED VISITORS

The Visitor Reception has been designed with disabled visitors in mind and provides full wheelchair access including toilet facilities. A special parking area is available near the Goods Shed to enable those with walking difficulties avoid the footbridge and a ramp is available to facilitate access to the passenger trains on operating days. Arrangements can be made to enable such visitors to reach many other parts of the Museum site, although certain areas, such as signal boxes, are likely to prove difficult or impossible in some cases. Please feel free to telephone the Museum on (01206) 242524 any day and discuss what we can do to make the visit of yourself and your party as easy as possible.

EDUCATIONAL FACILITIES

The Museum is a registered educational charity. As such its prime aim is to spread knowledge and interpretation of the railway history of East Anglia. We aim to relate our collection to the changing social and economic conditions during the past as well as tracing the progress in engineering matters. We are host to many visits from schools and other young groups and offer support to teachers by way of a series of information sheets on various topics and other material for specific requirements. The Museum's Board Room can be made available for lectures. We can tailor such visits to meet the requirements of National Curriculum courses. For further details please ask for our Education Sheet at the Booking Office or telephone our Education Officer on (01206) 242524.

FUTURE PLANS

Schemes for improvements to the Museum site are many and varied with some only being at a very early planning stage as yet. As today's news is tomorrow's history, our collection is continually evolving. We have disposed of to other preservation organisations some items of rolling stock that were not typical of East Anglia, and we will continue to try and demonstrate the rich history of railways throughout East Anglia over the past one hundred and fifty years.

Since the foundation of the Museum in 1968, we have learnt that there is a lot more to the operation of trains than just their purchase. The Restoration shed has been built to provide quality under cover facilities for the restoration and repair of locomotives, carriages and wagons. Development of a new carriage shed is actively under way, so that when carriages and wagons have been restored to a high standard they can be protected from the elements. We also need to improve the facilities for our visitors and plans are continually being developed and actioned to do so.

Whilst the income from admission charges (which are subject to VAT, so the Inland Revenue take their cut) and from the shop and catering pay for the day to day operation of the Museum, we depend on the support of our members for its development and long term future. Whilst we do have one full time and one part-time employee, everyone else associated with the Museum is a volunteer member. We welcome all new members, whether they wish to be actively involved or not. Please ask at the Visitor Reception for further details, visit our web site at http://www.earm.co.uk or telephone 01206 242524 for more information.

FURTHER READING

The following publications are available from the Station Bookshop:-

1. The Stour Valley Railway by B.D.J. Walsh. This provides a definitive history of the Stour Valley Railway line running from Marks Tey to Shelford, with a branch from Long Melford to Bury St. Edmunds. Gradient diagrams, sample fares and track layouts of the stations are all included along with a wealth of facts and figures and a fine collection of photographs. A chapter covering the preservation era has been added bringing the story right up to date with the line now terminating at Sudbury. A new edition is in course of preparation.

2. East Anglian Railway Museum Stock Book gives detailed information on current items of rolling stock at the Museum, and is fully illustrated. A new edition will be available in late Summer 2004.

A wide selection of transport books is stocked by the Bookshop, including histories of other local lines, such as Dennis Swindale's 'Branch Lines to Maldon' and 'Branch Line to Southminster', and Carl Lombardelli's 'Branch Lines to Braintree'. Please telephone the Bookshop Manager on 01206 242524.

Thank you for visiting please come again – and tell your family and friends about the East Anglian Railway Museum.

On a number of days each year the Museum's demonstration freight train operates, giving visitors the chance to ride in an open wagon or cattle van.

EAST ANGLIAN RAILWAY MUSEUM GUIDE BOOK
ISBN 0950647314

This edition has been compiled by Mark Cornell, Mark House, Ian Brown and Mike Stanbury, with help from many other Museum members with both information and photographs.